HOW TO GET RID OF YOUR STUFF (CRAP) AND TURN IT INTO CASH!
(Get rid of your unwanted items while fattening your wallet with yard and garage sales!)

By
Domenic Costa

Introduction

I make $400. minimum and more from my yard sales! Often it's more, much more! I do this once a month from my garage and/or driveway. You can get rid of your unwanted and underused household/work items easily and put some cash in your pocket! You can do it! Here's the Chapter Titles to guide you and help you make that money!

Chapter 1

GET RID OF THAT STUFF AND MAKE THAT MONEY NOW!

WE ARE A NATION OF CONSUMERS IN THE UNITED STATES! From birth until death, we are bombarded with messages to purchase and buy things in the United States of America to appear and feel well not only with ourselves, but also amongst our peers! We are a nation of hoarders and pack rats who have even, by necessity, created a multibillion-dollar industry specializing in storage. Maybe it's the holiday or Christmas season and you have this entire new bunch of product that needs to be put away, but you have all of your old gear taking up room in your dwelling. It's time to clean out your old and under-used stuff to make room for your new things. Maybe your children have outgrown their bedroom set, toys, clothes, and baby stuff! It's got to go! I am also a firm believer that the things we own can begin to own us in terms of our time, money and focus. Having less means we have less to fix, store, maintain, etc… Reducing the number of things in our lives that take our precious time can free you up to spend your time on this planet more focused on the things you really should be focusing on! Some of those things may be your mental state (make it better), relationships (family, spouse, life-partner, etc…), career, financial gain and stability and many more!

I have never seen moving trucks follow a hearse to the cemetery! They don't dig bigger holes for your coffin for all of the items you have acquired over a lifetime. When we die, we take NOTHING with us! ABSOLUTELY NOTHING! Holding on to things you do not use for many years that you have to pay to store and maintain takes your money away from the type of life you may want to live. A life where you live big and give big! Living big could be experiences with great relationships, travel, eating well, etc... Giving big can be to your favorite charitable organizations or your own personal ones! How about just giving a huge tip during the holidays to your favorite service workers and watch the joy in their faces! Or you could go to your favorite restaurant and buy meals for strangers! The list of giving big is endless with lots of joy to be given and received!

You can psychologically heal yourself by letting unused or little-used items go. I am not talking about tools. They can be held for a lifetime of benefit. We need to learn to declutter our lives. We have to learn to get rid of that stuff! We have to learn to be ready to let it go bye-bye! Here are some examples of the cost of holding on to that stuff!

I often go to storage unit auctions to acquire more product/stuff to sell at my yard sales. While there, I talk with people I meet and I often find people who are trying to get rid of stuff in their storage units to unburden themselves of the rental obligation for the unit. That's how I met the gentlemen who gave us the baby unit. He and his wife had two sons, now ages 9 and 11. When the boys were 2 and 4, the little family had moved and had put into storage most, if not all of their children's clothes, toys, etc... For the past 7 years (84+ months) they had been paying around $200.00 per month for this stuffed locker. They had spent enough money to buy a brand new Toyota Corolla with what they had spent maintaining a unit chock full of stuff that should have been sold at a yard sale seven years prior! The items in that unit were not worth $16,800.00! My son and I emptied his unit and sold everything in there for a little over $300.00 and gave away a bunch to some young families in need. Sell your stuff people! Let it go! Use your money, in this case, to do better things for you, your family, for others, and retirement!

Another two units acquired in a similar way was from the Anglo American lady who had fallen in love with a Japanese man 28 years earlier and had packed most of her apartment into two storage lockers when she married the guy moving to Japan as well. After staying married to the same gentleman for over 28 years she decided it was finally time to let that stuff go! All she wanted from those units was a Waterford crystal vase (made in Ireland) and two original watercolor paintings. Now it is true that those three items, especially the art work, could have gained or retained tremendous value, but to pay for 28 years (336 months) for two units at around $150 a month for both comes to somewhere about $50,400.00! Wow! The residual stuff in those units only sold for almost $600.00. I hope it's becoming clear that we've got to make better decisions with our money!

My final story is about a singer who left everything and moved to San Diego, California from Torrance, California after giving 15 years of her life attempting to become a big time singer in Los Angeles, California. She contacted me after she could not sell her stuff at the storage facility all that well. Her stuff was well packed in her 5' by 10' room and it was hard to dig items out of her unit for her by appointment only "yard sale" at the storage facility. Fortunately for her, she had not carried her unit for as long as the other two mentioned and it was really a wise move on her part to disengage herself from this "stuff" so she could make a fresh start in San Diego as a house sitter no less! Her 15-year battle to make it in the music biz had taken a personal toll on her private and public lives and she really wanted to get rid of her stuff and get that new and fresh start! I appreciated that I could help by claiming her items and freeing up her budget of having to pay a monthly storage fee for items that were of no use to her anymore. Some were given away and the rest were sold for a tidy profit for my own goals.

The following chapters are arranged by highest to lowest price you can expect to receive for your items.

Chapter 2

Sell the Unusual Good Stuff on eBay!

Yes, I know eBay is changing even at the time of this writing and yes; their fees make me shake my head! You cannot deny their global viewership for your more special or popular items (translate-- the more expensive Good Stuff!). Their global reach is huge and Impressive and I have to give them proper due and respect for allowing me to attempt to sell my items on their platform. If you have collectibles, high-end electronics, designer labeled clothing, vintage kitchen/cookware/dining items, then this is the place to get the biggest bang for your buck.

EBay is very time consuming, so it behooves you to get a sense of what you have to sell and its value. This means that you've got to go on eBay and spend some time researching the value of your item(s). You will do this by typing the name of your item into the search box and clicking search when you are on the eBay site. Once your results pop in and trust me, there may be many, I go to the left column and click on sold listings, not the completed listings. I want to learn what my items are actually selling for presently. This will let me determine if it is worth my time (you will have to determine this on your own what your price point is) to even list them. If I will be listing over 25 items, then I will not mind having some items that net less than $10. My rule of thumb for eBay is the items must net out after eBay and PayPal fees a minimum of $10 per item to justify my time that I will spend doing my research, listing, shipping, mailing, answering questions from potential buyers, and leaving feedback as well as handling possible returns. As I do this more and more, as of this writing, I am currently heading towards a $15 plus price point. You are going to have to join eBay and PayPal to get started on listing and getting paid too. That means you have to have a bank savings/checking account as well as a credit card.

Prepare yourself for the fees! EBay charges a listing fee per item (often they have no listing fees as a come-on or as a seasonal promotion), a percentage of your selling price is claimed and a percentage of the shipping cost if you use eBay to print out your postage. PayPal charges another fee based on your sale price! It's not free or cheap! It feels to me about 15-20% of what they bite out is from your total sales. On the other hand though, eBay still has the biggest market presence closely followed by Amazon. If you are willing to ship internationally, you will truly increase your breadth and scope of potential buyers for your items!

To get my listings on quick and easy, I use the eBay app on my iPhone. It let's a "Baby Boomer" like myself easily and quickly take pictures, write the listing, figure in the way I'm going to ship it, and get paid. To attract more interest and buyers, I offer free shipping for just about all of my items. This will factor into your asking price as well. People LOVE FREE SHIPPING!

Another eBay tip is that I typically forgo listing any of my things with auctions starting at 99 cents and lately; I have had a lot of success by setting my price and listing it for Best Offer. As long as I've priced it right (all labor and shipping costs), then I will accept most if not all offers that are at least 66% plus of my starting price. Remember, I want to sell as much as possible. Whatever I don't sell on eBay I will invariably let go for the low, low price at my yard/garage sale. So be ready to accept those offers and Get Rid of That Stuff! The 99-cent starting price auctions with no reserve (this means you WILL sell it at whatever price it gets when your auction closes), I will do only for popular items that may blow through the roof in terms of final price and bidding action. You have got to do your research on Sold listings to determine if this is the best way to get some potentially big payoffs for your "hot" items! Some items that sold big for me were game systems, games, autographed items (Elizabeth Taylor), sports memorabilia (O.J. Simpson), some designer clothes and (Gucci sunglasses) accessories, etc... The more you use eBay, the better you will get at discerning what will sell best and by what format to get you your best price for your item(s). Remember, you are selling it ultimately to declutter your life and to make money for your next adventure!

Once you have buyers making offers that you have accepted, then get ready to get paid by immediately invoicing them. If they do not pay after 24 hours, then invoice them again. If after 2 days they have not paid, send them a note through eBay that you will file an unpaid item case for not paying you against them if they do not pay after 72 hours (3 days is the time frame for Best Offer sales on eBay). Don't get mad at buyers! Check out my YouTube video: (https://www.youtube.com/watch?v=5ykgQ90tWSY&list=PLYPn0S qDBpCoalowpREpfIluijj8ELkpl&index=2).

Getting mad is a waste of your energy in this case! Stay calm and file your unpaid cases. If the buyer does not pay, simply re-list when eBay closes the case. Most buyers do not want one of these cases against them. Do not make the mistake of getting excited and packaging your item and purchasing postage through eBay without the client paying first. Get paid first, and then take care of buying postage, boxing/wrapping your item, and then leaving positive feedback to your buyer who paid ever so promptly!

Here are some more things to remember about eBay: get to know the rules of the site, be professional, be patient, and be honest. Take good pictures and lots of pictures as well. Currently, my eBay app allows 12 pictures for each listing for FREE! Pictures tell the story about your item way better than words ever could! For most items, I take my pictures with a white towel or blanket for a backdrop. I have no other items in the picture to distract the attention from the item I am selling. The fluorescent lighting in my listing room seems to work best. Make sure your photos have little or no glare or shadows in them. Many smart phones have great cameras built in and this is what I use for all of my eBay listings. The camera is easy to use and with a bit of practice you will be able to produce great, well-lit pictures that will help entice and sell your item. You must write good and clear descriptions with precise measurements. I often photograph a ruler/meter stick next to my items to help with this as well. Items, once sold, must be packed with care! Do not skimp on this! Dealing with items that broke during shipping will cause you grief in terms of time, material, and money! Be aware that all sellers are required to have a return policy. If I have sold an item for over $100, I always purchase the insurance when shipping that item as well. This will help with breakage or loss. Tracking numbers are provided for your items when you ship through eBay. If you can't prove it got to your buyer's location, you will have to send another or issue a full refund. Some buyers are scammers and occasionally try to rip you off by saying the item didn't arrive or perhaps it arrived broken. Tracking numbers and insurance can help with this aspect of selling and help you keep that stuff going out as you collect that cash with minimal headaches. Sell away!!!!

I personally ship most of my items with USPS Priority Mail. I get the boxes and envelopes from my local post office or I have them delivered to my house for FREE by placing my order online to the USPS. That is pretty cool! Brown paper grocery bags acquired for free when I shop can be used to wrap your items or packages. I find huge amounts of clean and FREE bubble wrap in a dumpster behind some local businesses on my daily drive home from work too! You are going to ship stuff when you use eBay and any way you can save your dollars as far as I'm concerned is a good thing! Another way I have discovered to sell on eBay is with local pick up, which really is free shipping for you the seller! Items that are sold this way are actually picked up at your location by the buyer! Items I sell this way are typically over-sized and heavy items that would be difficult for the average person to package and ship. Antique furniture pieces as well as large signs can be sold this way with great success. One thing I recommend is to put a number of days and (or) week(s) limit that the buyer has to come and pick it up after they have paid completely for the item. This will free you up to resell the item either on eBay or on another selling platform (Craigslist perhaps!).

Chapter 3

Sell the Good Stuff and the Stuff with Barcodes on Amazon!

I love Amazon! They make it easy to list, ship, and get paid for your items! I use Amazon specifically for any item that has a barcode. By simply punching in the number listed with the barcode into Amazon (Amazon Seller Central), I am shown if this item is available for sale on Amazon and what the current asking price for it is, whether it is new or used. If it is profitable to sell, you simply click the link to sell your item and it will take you to a page where you simply fill it in and with a handful or less of clicks your item is listed onto Amazon's worldwide platform!

Here is the story of how I got started with Amazon on YouTube:(https://www.youtube.com/watch?v=dS-jBaA9yOw), "3000 Books In Spanish And Why Coach Dom Sells Stuff On Amazon!!!" is the title of this video and the lessons I learned changed my selling life forever! After having bought an abandoned storage locker with unbeknownst to me over 3000 brand new fiction books written in the Spanish language in it! I at that time no platform to sell them on until I began to do my research and that is when I took the plunge and opened my own Amazon account and linked it to one of my checking accounts. I listed over 90 of the books in the first week and after a month of selling I had sold...0 books!!! I was not deterred! I began my research in earnest and I was able to find the only 3 resellers of books written in Spanish in the great big city of Los Angeles, California and was able to sell ALL of the books for a miniscule profit! I was not too worried because I had learned a valuable lesson. I had discovered the selling platform of Amazon! Within a year I totaled up right around $900 in profit/sales from my account! I used to wonder if I was selling my DVD's too cheaply before this at my yard sales when buyers would swoop them up en masse. Well I was! Thanks to Amazon, I input every book, DVD, cd, toy, or any item with a barcode into my Amazon seller account and I sell it. It has become a nice income stream for me and it can help you get a better price for your bar-coded items as you sell them and reduce the clutter in your life! Start an Amazon account now!

The fees at Amazon are smaller than eBay and what they include for shipping (that the customer pays) almost always is generous enough that I cover my shipping costs with a small profit as well. They are a huge company with a large reach and platform on the world's stage for your items. There is no PayPal or their fees! Your profits are deposited to you every 2 weeks. It has been easy for me and I believe it will be easy for you!

Chapter 4

Sell the OK and the Big Heavy Stuff on Craigslist!

I love Craigslist!!!! Yes, there are weirdos out there, but I have been very successful selling my in-between items that would/could not sell on eBay or Amazon. These items sold on Craigslist got me way more money than if I had sold them at my typical blow-it-all-out yard sale. Craigslist has allowed me the opportunity to advertize my items for FREE! That's right, FREE! This is the future! My Smartphone Craigslist app (http://itunes.apple.com/app/id310947683) allows me to quickly and easily list my item with up to 24 pictures taken by the same Smartphone. I won't talk about buying things on Craigslist for amazing prices and then later reselling them for a profit-that may be the topic or chapter title for another book!

Here are some tips:
1. Repost or renew your ads regularly to keep your ad on top of the listings page in Craigslist. Buyers don't want to go through pages of old listings. You have to make it easy for your buyers to find your item and you! In Los Angeles, California where I live, ads can be renewed every 48 hours. Ads in Los Angeles, California Craigslist expire after 7 days and in other cities it will be 30 or more days. By putting your items in ads in different categories, you will get more exposure to your buyers and increase your sales. Having multiple ads under different categories will allow you to have ads up in case for some strange reason somebody decides to mark your ad as SPAM and marks it for automatic removal off of Craigslist. I don't know why people will SPAM your ad but it happens. No worries though, you have multiple ads and exposure still available for your future purchasing public! I will put my ads for items up Day 1 under one category, and Day 2 under another. This will allow me to renew/repost my listings on a daily basis. If my ads do not get a

response or a sale in 7 days, I will not hesitate to lower my price in all of my ads for that particular item until I sell it. If it does not sell by the time of my yard sale, I will remove my ads and sell at my yard sale! I have Craigslist manners, too! It really helps my life from responding to unneeded calls, texts, and emails by simply, easily, and courteously removing all of my ads for that item once I have sold it or it is now going to be in my yard sale.

2. Always post great pictures! Great pictures are like the old saying that a picture is worth a thousand words! They really can show the detail of your item and is the best way of showing how it looks without actually being in the item's presence. Humans are visual creatures. The vast majority of people will click on image-based ads only! Currently in Los Angeles, California, Craigslist will let you post up to 24 pictures per ad! This will truly illuminate your item(s) for sale! I will especially use all 24 pictures for my yard/garage sale ads to literally show all of the items on top of my display tables and everything set under my display tables! Check your pictures! Make sure the flash hasn't over-exposed your items. I have found that my pictures for eBay and Amazon look great with a white background. If it is a possibility, try to photograph your items with a light or white background provided by a towel, sheet of paper, or a large drop cloth.

3. Be specific in your title! Keep your title purely informational. Remember that you are trying to sell something that people will have to go out of their way to purchase. People want to know as much as possible about the item before they spend the time and gas money to travel to your home or place of business. Make it easy to find your item with a specific title!

4. Do your Double D's (not those)! Double D's is an acronym for "Due Diligence" in my world. This means that you spend the time or do your homework to see what is selling on Craigslist and for what price. Spend some quality time looking at similar items you are trying to sell on Craigslist. Search the ads; see what similar items are selling for. Do you see an item that has been posted up over and over? Can you guess why it hasn't sold? Was it overpriced? What was wrong with it based on what you see in the pictures? Were the pictures of poor quality? Were there no pictures? Was the ad poorly written? Other ads will help you write your ads for your items as well as help you make a basic template for your ads with your contact information. Be prepared to get and sell your items for 20

25% less than what you listed them for. Build that into your pricing for your stuff. Hey folks, letting that stuff go is your mentality. Price accordingly and be prepared to make your buyers feel like they are getting a GREAT deal! Craigslist is the last rung of my sales ladder to get a better price and therefore more cash for my things!

5. Cash only! Cash only! Cash only! Twenty dollar bills or smaller is preferred (less counterfeiting in this money range) is what I prefer to make change for my customers.

6. Pair up items that go together like tables and chairs, desk and chair, crib and changing table, etc... The chances are that if someone is looking for one, they may need the other. Offer a discount for taking both and if need be, split the items to make any and all sales. Move that stuff!!

7. Craigslist buyers are impulse buyers for the most part! You greatly increase your chances for making a sale when you return any emails, texts, or calls immediately. Many buyers contact many sellers and will buy typically to the first seller that responds.

8. Consider trades or bartering! If there's an item or service you want that is as good as cash, add it to your post. You never know what pleasant or positive surprise awaits as you keep getting rid of that stuff.

9. WARNING!!!!! BE SAFE!!! Safety comes first when it comes to getting rid of your things and making that cash. Unlike eBay, where one-on-one meetings are unlikely, or at a crowded garage sale, Craigslist has an element of risk. I have sold hundreds of items and have not had one single problem but I am a male and that can play a part in that equation. I do not invite people into my home to see an item. I may invite them into my garage that is at the front of my house but that is about it. My sales are typically made outside of my home on my driveway or my covered entryway. My garage cabinets all have doors so what people can see is limited. Most, if not all of my sales, are done with at least a family member or friend, who if they are not with me selling the item, are in the home and are aware that I am outside in front of their locked and closed entry door making a sale. My advice is to communicate back and forth to clearly establish the intent of the buyer to buy. In my Craigslist ads, you can contact me by email, text, or phone call. All methods have worked well as forms of communication but direct phone calls has been by far the strongest signal I have used to establish the seriousness of the buyer to purchase. It may be good to get their

whole name if you wish to Google them as well to get more information before establishing a meet time if need be. Remember to always be safe!

10. BE CAREFUL! I carry as little change as possible and keep it in my pockets to make change fast and to close the sale even faster! There is nothing like watching the red tail lights of your buyer's vehicle drive away as you feel the cash in hand and being flushed with the knowledge that you have gotten rid of one more item you will not have to move, store, pack, or worry about again!

Chapter 5
Blow Out Everything Else at Your Yard and Garage Sales!

You now have tried to sell anything you perceive of value with eBay, Amazon, Craigslist and any other venue you can think of. If you haven't sold it by now, then it is time to get your mind on point to let all that other stuff GO at your yard/garage sale! You have to get over yourself and get this stuff gone! Get your seller's mindset ready! That's the key! Be ready to blow it all out and sell it all!! We are not going to get retail prices at our yard sales! A yard sale or garage sale (depending on your venue) is the more traditional and oldest form of clearing out your stuff! Sell it all! The following paragraphs and bullets will demonstrate my methodology and tips of my sales to turn your castoffs into cash!

Do you live where you need a permit or license to have a sale? In some gated communities it is a big no to having a sale! Sometimes the sales are limited to a certain weekend of the year. Find out what is available in your area and go forth once you know you have the green light to go and have your blow out sale from wherever you live.

Another great idea is to see if your neighbors want to also have a "block type" sale to attract visitors. I let my immediate neighbors know I am going to have a sale for just this reason. I share with them all of the ways I have advertized publicly for my sale and they have seen my BIG signs too. They know it is easy to piggyback on my advertizing blitz and that they can also put out a few items on their driveways and make a few dollars as well without spending a nickel on advertizing! Even if they don't sell anything, they will be mentally prepared for the noise and traffic on a Saturday morning. They seem to appreciate the fact that I am courteous, forthright, and especially that my sales end often around 11am and that everything is done by 12 noon.

If you are doing this out of your home, you need to check your homeowner's insurance! Strangers will be on your property walking around. Make sure your sale layout is safe and easy to move around in. I have a number of fold up tables for family and friend gatherings that I use for my sales as well. I keep them separated for ease of customer movement. If your stuff is stacked up, then be safe in how you stack it and lay it out. Display everything neatly and individually so customers don't have to dig through boxes. I keep an electrical power strip handy so my electric items can be tested but I keep an eye on it so no one uses it in a way or fashion where they may be shocked! Keep your pets away from the sale! Some people may be afraid or they may get scratched or worse, bit! Keep your small children away as well because they may distract you or your customers to cause an unsafe condition. Safety is and should be #1 at all times! Do not be negligent in your layout of your sale items! Be safe! Keep your customers safe!

Do you live in a gated community? Do you live in a condominium complex? Do you live in an apartment building? If you say yes to any of those questions, then you will have to find out if having a sale is even allowed. If the answer is no, then don't worry! I have heard of sellers moving their sale to a friend's home where there are no restrictions for a yard sale. Yes, it is more work to move all of your stuff to another location, but it is better to put out the energy to get rid of your crap/stuff and to make a little money as well than to believe you are stuck and cannot have a sale to get rid of things and make a little cash!

Should you use newspaper ads or not? It's your call! The largest percentage of buyers for my sales gets the information about my sales from my multiple free Craigslist ads. These are the buyers that spend the most money as well. My newspaper ad buyers typically do not buy as much my other buyers. It has made financial sense to skip the expensive newspaper ads versus the free ads placed online.

Advertise! You must create awareness that you are doing this sale to get customers there to buy your stuff and put money in your pocket! I like free ads! Put an ad in the free classified ads' newspaper or mailer in your locale. Put signs in the stores that allow it in your neighborhood like Laundromats or Starbucks, which often have community billboards. I absolutely love putting my sale ads on Craigslist for zero cost. If you are on various social media like Facebook you can let the world know as well about your sale. Facebook also has local groups on their site dedicated to sales where you live. Consider joining these groups or finding out if you can post your sale information on their group pages to get more of your local buyers to visit and or purchase at your sale extravaganza. Some sellers will post flyers around their neighborhood on street sign poles as well as power poles to advertise their sale! (Be a good neighbor though and please remove your signs after the sale!!! Don't provide the blight in your neighborhood!)

If you do these sales often, I highly recommend starting an email or phone list. Ask customers to sign up at your sale and promise not to group text them the sale information or email them any ads for men's hair care products. I will typically hold a presale for this large group of buyers the day before my actual sale. Yes, they will buy the good stuff, but that is all right because I will be able to get a higher price for those items in my presales than I will at my regularly scheduled yard sale. To stay sane, I will schedule my presale for only a limited amount of time. It usually is a 2 to 3 hour window like 4 to 7pm.

I set up my yard sale in the days prior to the presale on folding tables in my garage. On the day of my big sale, if the weather allows, I prefer that my sale be outdoors on my driveway so I can get people out of my garage for safety and security reasons. If it rains, we will stay in the garage, but you have to keep a sharp eye out on people because they will start opening cabinets and start to load their vehicles with your personal non-sellable stuff! I will ask my early bird customers to actually help me physically pick up and move my merchandise-loaded tables with me onto my driveway. They will earn a discount of course! It is a relief to be able to shut my garage door and to secure my personal stuff.

Many sellers put price tags or removable stickers on their items and that can be a great thing. I have also seen it be a turn off for buyers! Remember that this is a blow out sale and that NO offer should be refused and that NO customer should leave your sale without an item in his or her hand! You do not want to repack this stuff! It needs to get gone! With this in mind, it always a good idea to check all of your sale area and tables before any selling begins to double-check that no items of value have made their way out to your sale where they may be snatched up and be gone forever!

My official times for my yard sales are 7am to 11am. You can count on me though to be up and eating breakfast by 5:45am. While I am eating, I repost my yard/garage sale ads for Craigslist with my Craigslist app on my Smartphone so that when all the yard/garage hunters get up, they will see my ad for my sale on the top of the listings page and if not, then very close to the top and on the front page for that search at the least! Before I go to my garage to open up by 6am, I get a big thermos full of coffee ready and a couple of granola bars ready to go with me. I will be on my feet moving and burning calories at a pretty good pace for the next 3 hours solid without a break. You have got to stay hydrated and fed properly to keep your energy up during this peak selling time! (Thankfully my wife or one of my kids will step in to give me some supervision help by 9am so I can take a bathroom break!) After stepping into my attached garage, I put on my Home Depot bought and low cost, around-the-waist canvas nail/screw pouch with all of my money in there for change and payment. I put my fully charged cell phone into my pant's pocket, place a hat on my head to stay warm and keep the sun's rays off of my shaved dome, and head out into the day. I will get my Yard sale signs and head to my ¼ of a block away parked truck (it is parked on a nearby thoroughfare). My signs are BIG!!! Check out my three helpful videos on YouTube:
(https://www.youtube.com/watch?v=Mbz2kdN3_U4&index=2&list
=PLYPn0SqDBpCqz
T547DkyneaZTLU5I9u5g),
(https://www.youtube.com/watch?v=9KYWJKiOlT4&list=PLYPn0
SqDBpCqzT547Dky
neaZTLU5I9u5g&index=3), and
(https://www.youtube.com/watch?v=V7FLnvN0daQ&index=4&list
=PLYPn0SqDBpCqz
T547DkyneaZTLU5I9u5g).

Big ugly signs attract attention and money! At my truck, I place my signs out as well as my traffic cones and traffic barrier with the huge arrow on it pointing to my yard sale location. I will then head back to my garage and get out my traffic barricade horse with the big FREE painted on it with the arrow on it and place it in the street near my house while I briskly move/schlep my predesignated FREE Items in their boxes in and around that FREE sign. (People LOVE FREE STUFF!) I have gained new customers for my list and also increased my sales with the FREE sign! People will break their necks to stop for a FREE sign and consequently while they are out of their cars will stop and have a look-see at the other items at your sale. I make sure they leave with something they pay for and if not, it is no big deal because I make a point to get their contact information so I can notify them of my next sale as well as find out what they are currently looking for. The bottom line is I am gaining a new customer as well as moving out product that I will not have to expend the energy again to repack and move again. Believe me when I tell you that I am mentally prepared for all of this stuff to go from my house to another. My goal is to have the smallest amount of leftovers or no leftovers at all after my sale!!

All of this work is done before 7am because I love early birds! Early birds typically show up any where from 30 to 45 minutes before the official start time of your sale. Be ready for them. These are usually your swap meet and flea market sellers who want to pick up more inventory. They want the better stuff you have. Be ready for them and sell to them hard! They will pay more for items than the others that will show up after 7am. They want the goodies and you can demand and receive better prices for all of your items from the early birds! Be prepared!

Get enough change to keep your sales flowing! I have about $4 dollars in quarters, dimes, and nickels as well as $40 - $60 in mostly $1's and $5's U.S. dollars You can almost guarantee that some buyers will be breaking a $20 dollar bill for a $2 dollar purchase. Be ready and take their money and give them change. As the sale progresses throughout the day your cash pile will get thicker and you will have no problem giving change. In fact, when your buyers are making purchases with bigger bills, do not hesitate to ask if they have smaller denominations to help you out! A word of caution, be careful with larger U. S. denominations like $50. and $100. dollar bills. Many counterfeit bills are floating around and get laundered at yard sales! In fact, check all of your bills of all denominations when they come through your hands. Today's photocopiers and printers make great copies and people can be pretty underhanded! Don't be caught at the end of the day when you are counting your money and you discover the fake dollars that destroy your profits!

Keep your valuables on you at all times during your sale! That expensive cell phone needs to be on your person! Wear less jewelry too! An ostentatious looking seller at a yard sale may tip off thieves that you may be a location they might want to visit again when there is no sale and no one home. Be careful! If you are not comfortable dealing with a sale and the crowds that may come, then please arrange to have a friend or relative with you to help you, your items, and location be safe. More eyes have always been helpful for me to keep it safe!

When you complete sales, some buyers for your and their ease will ask to make a big pile of stuff/items from which you can then negotiate a final price. This is an easy way to move a large pile of your "get it gone" merchandise! Please go through the pile as you sell it, even if you know what lowball price you have in mind for the pile. Why, you might ask? Well, once again people/buyers can be underhanded and hide some of your more valuable items under the pile they are hoping you don't go through. (I know you sold the good stuff already on eBay, Amazon, Craigslist, etc… as well as at your presale!) Yes, they will hide better items in the bottom of the pile and or boxes and bags you provided. They will, but if you catch it, don't go nuts! Pull the expensive item or point it out and ask your potential customer if they were going to buy the item. No accusing goes on (stay safe and sane), only sales and deal making!

Have plenty of boxes and bags for your customers to put their purchased items in and to make it easy to leave your sale. Have newspaper available as well to wrap any breakable items. Make it as easy as possible for your customers to get it (their purchases) and get it gone! Our goal, as you remember, is to have zero products for you to pack up and move again. Sell it all!

Sale hours for me, as I mentioned is from 7am to 11 am. Depending on the crowds and what and how much is being sold, I will make a decision that if my sales are slow or most of my stuff has been sold, then after 9am I install my "Blow It All Out!!!!" pricing mentality on all of my items! My goal is to have little to nothing left! Go forth and sell it ALL kids!

Chapter 6

Scraps--What's Left and How to Get Rid of It Easy, Quick, and at Low or No Cost!

As I mentioned in the last chapter, my sales run from 7am to 11am. That's right, only 4 hours! I may stay at the latest until 12 noon if there is still some product to move and customers are there perusing and purchasing. In my experience though in my community/suburb of Los Angeles, California, is that most of the sellers and purchases have already happened. I have stayed late into the afternoon and sold $2.00 worth of stuff in 1 hour. For me that is not a good use of time and prolongs my cleanup and moving on to my next exciting activity of the day. So if things are slowing down in, on, or around 11 am, I start to break down my sale. Actually, I've been doing that in a way throughout the sale by continually re-displaying items on my tables and driveway as items were purchased. Towards the end of my sales, there is less stuff to sell so I may even have collapsed some of my folding tables to ease and quicken my final shutdown. Once I have committed to the fact that the sale is over, I simply put all of my leftover/unsold items into boxes and bags and I place them on my parkway or curb with a "Free" sign. I use my Craigslist app on my Smartphone and list all of it on the Craigslist Free section with plenty of pictures. I make sure that my address is clearly noted and I also explain that I have Craigslist manners. Craigslist manners are where I simply state that my ad will stay up as long as there are free items that are available to be picked up. I have not made one dump run in all of my years of selling. It's true! People have taken EVERYTHING over 90% of the time. The last 10% maybe of such low quality that I may simply put it in my municipal trash and recycle bins or if there is any good stuff, I will make a short run to Goodwill to get a charitable donation receipt or I will drop the rest into many or any of the charitable collection bins that are near where

I live. EVERYTHING and I mean EVERYTHING is gone in 12 to 24 hours! Now is the time to begin enjoying your new open space and decluttered life as well as counting that cash!!!

Chapter 7
How This All Started--Josephine's Story

This journey of having yard sales began with an event that happened while at work. I am a 30+ year high school science teacher. The majority of my students the school year this takes place in mostly consisted of 9th graders in my Integrated Coordinated Science classes. My school at that time had kids from low to moderate/middle income families. 9th graders (14 to 15 years old) at a grade 9 through 12 school are very energetic as they go on the puberty conveyor belt to adolescence and adulthood and can be very immature at times as well. The majority are, for the most part, beautiful human beings who cannot control themselves that well yet because their brains haven't caught up with their amped up hormonal bodies.

Josephine was a member of my classes. She, like so many other of the students, had a cell phone. This was at the time when iPhones had been around for about 2 years and were very popular with all of their abilities. Not everyone had one because they or their families could not afford one. Josephine was part of this group and had an older model flip phone. On this day, during the class group activities I was monitoring, she was bemoaning the fact that she could not get one of those phones because she was broke and being 14 she wasn't even old enough in Los Angeles, California to even attempt to get a work permit to work at your typical minimum wage fast food institution or store, (You have to be 16 to get one!). This caught my attention, because in my experience of being raised by a self-employed building contractor and his bookkeeping wife, you could make way more than minimum wage by hustling and providing a service for others. All of this could be done at ANY age without a work permit! I stopped the class and shared this "Biology of Life" story that I would challenge her "I can't afford it" mindset by showing how I would make money with NO or little money!

This is where the journey began for my first book: "Hustling for

Cash Money With Metal Recycling!!!
(http://www.amazon.com/dp/B00FF1VF1W/ref=rdr_kindle_ext_tm)
I turned a $25 start-up investment to over 3k in about 12 months! I did this while sharing this journey with all of my classes. My moneymaking hustling activities consisted of a mix of storage auction resales, metal recycling, Craigslist Free resales, small hustle/labor jobs, and of course, yard sales! These were all done as examples for the kids. This "Biology of Life" story nearly always had a student or two in each class share their service or opportunistic story of their "hustling" escapades. Their money making endeavors ranged from babysitting, yard sales, washing/detailing cars, yard work, housecleaning, selling on EBay the Christmas Lenox ornaments their Mom was going to throw away, helping senior citizens with chores, etc… Yes we did cover our "California State Standards for Science", but we also shared our "Biology of Life" of acquiring the mindset and vision to attempt to earn the money to get that better cell phone, provide for your needs, provide for your family, or help others. A big thank you goes to "Josephine" whose story has inspired many a conversation in many classes since that time to go out, see what you want, get off your butt, plan, act decisively, and get what you want in life! Life is a short ride with an end--get moving kids!!!

Conclusion

I used to worry in my past life what others thought of me or if they giggled or snickered at why a grown-ass professional is now the King of Yard Sales in their neighborhood. I don't care and I love it!!!! I laugh as I keep stacking that cash and provide for my loved ones and achieve bit by bit my financial and life goals. The students in my classes dig the stories and YouTube videos. Their newfound "Hustles" inspire me as I have hoped I have inspired them as well. In fact I have found that most of the people in my life are encouraging of my efforts and most importantly my family is cheering me on as I/we enjoy the fruits of my labor! Here's to you and your journey! Get rid of that stuff and make that money!! This life is a short ride!!!! Let's roll!!!!

Salute!
Best wishes and luck!
Domenic Costa

P.S.-I'd love your comments, reviews, and critiques! Leave them here or contact me at:
dcosta1smallhaul@gmail.com.
You can find me on Twitter as well and here's the link:
(https://twitter.com/CostaDomenic)
I have quite a few YouTube videos too on this book's topic that I know you'll find informative and helpful as well! I have a special playlist with lots of videos on my Yard and Garage Sale adventures. They are informative and inspiring! (Well I like to think so! LOL!) Check them out!! Here's the link:
https://www.youtube.com/playlist?list=PLYPn0SqDBpCqzT547Dky neaZTLU5I9u5g
Or simply type in Coach Dom Costa in the search box at YouTube and search away! You will find me! I've been blessed and married to

my beautiful bride for over 25+ years and I can/want any input to get better! Thank you so much and happy selling!!!

Acknowledgements

A big, big thank you to my wife Pamela and my children, Lauren and Jacob, for all of your love, support, editing skills, and inspiration on Daddy's many adventures! I also want to thank Glendon Cameron for the Hustling and Creating inspiration (check him out on YouTube, and Facebook). A BIG note of thanks to you for choosing this book and taking a chance on my recipe for success! This is my big thank you as well for reading this book all the way to the end. If you have liked what you have read please take a moment to leave a review for this book on Amazon: http://www.amazon.com/dp/B00KVL5HYC

FTC